PERFECT
NEGOTIATION

Terry O'Brien is a best-selling author, columnist, consultant and motivational trainer. He is highly sought-after in the corporate as well as academic world, and has been training managers and providing counselling and consultancy over the past couple of decades. Author of hugely popular books on motivation, effective change and all that is 'un-Google-able', his writings focus on skill development and communication techniques. Terry O'Brien is a firm believer that 'infotainment' is a must for content to be effective, and his books are all about the three 'R's: Read, Record and Recall.

OTHER TITLES IN THE SERIES

Perfect Appraisal

Perfect Assertiveness

Perfect Communication

Perfect CV

Perfect Interview

Perfect Leader

Perfect Management Skills

Perfect Marketing

Perfect Meeting

Perfect People Skills

Perfect Personality

Perfect Presentation

Perfect Salesmanship

Perfect Strategy

Perfect Time Management

PERFECT
NEGOTIATION

Get it right every time

Terry O'Brien

RUPA

Published by
Rupa Publications India Pvt. Ltd 2017
7/16, Ansari Road, Daryaganj
New Delhi 110002

Sales centres:
Allahabad Bengaluru Chennai
Hyderabad Jaipur Kathmandu
Kolkata Mumbai

ISBN: 978-81-291-4540-6

First impression 2017

10 9 8 7 6 5 4 3 2 1

Typeset by Chetan Sharma

Contents

Introduction   *vii*

1. Stages of negotiation   1

2. Phases of negotiation   9

3. Styles of negotiation   58

4. Role of ploys   72

5. Negotiating disputes   82

Introduction

Negotiation is a method by which people settle differences. It is a process by which a compromise or an agreement is reached while avoiding arguments and disputes. In any disagreement, individuals understandably aim to achieve the best possible outcome for their position or perhaps an organisation they represent. However, the principles of fairness, seeking mutual benefit and maintaining a relationship are the keys to a successful outcome.

Specific forms of negotiation are used in different situations: international affairs, legal system, government, industrial disputes or domestic relationships. However, general negotiation skills can be learned and applied in a wide range of activities. Negotiation skills can be of great benefit in resolving any differences that arise between you and others.

It is inevitable! From time to time, conflict and disagreement will arise as the differing needs, wants, aims and beliefs of people are brought together. Without negotiation, such conflicts may lead to arguments and resentment, resulting in one or all of the parties feeling dissatisfied. The point of negotiation is to try to reach an agreement without causing future barriers to communication.

In order to achieve a desirable outcome, it may be useful to follow a structured approach to negotiation. For example, at work, a meeting may need to be arranged in which all parties involved can come together.

The process of negotiation includes: preparation, discussion, clarification of goals, negotiating towards a win-win outcome and reacting an agreement.

A negotiation is a communication process in which multiple parties discuss problems and attempt to solve them via dialogue in order to reach a solution. Negotiations occur constantly on micro and macro scales, both in the workplace and in everyday life. You are sure to encounter numerous types of negotiations as part of your daily tasks, such as salary negotiations, contract negotiations with outside counsel, settlement negotiations during litigation, union negotiations, purchase order negotiations, and more. There are advantages and disadvantages of different types of negotiating formats and styles, preparation strategies. This book would help one to equip oneself with the nuances of negotiation, however, the book makes little claim to originality or depth; it is based on the premise of experience and learning.

Indeed, here is all you need to get it right every time!

1

Stages Of Negotiation

Before any negotiation, a decision needs to be taken as to when and where a meeting will take place to discuss the problem and who will attend. Setting a limited time-frame for negotiations can also be helpful to prevent the disagreement from continuing.

This stage involves ensuring all the pertinent facts of the situation are known in order to clarify your own position. This would include knowing the 'rules' of your organisation. Your organisation may well have policies to which you can refer in preparation for the negotiation.

Preparation before discussing the points of disagreement will help to avoid further conflict and unnecessarily wasting time during the meeting.

There are several steps to take in the process of preparation.

- First, know what you want and don't want.
- Second, know what your counterpart wants and doesn't want.
- Third, identify possible concessions.
- Fourth, know the alternatives.
- Fifth, know the counterpart and subject matter.
- Sixth, rehearse.

Preparation, or lack of it, will become immediately apparent as negotiations get under way. A negotiator who arrives poorly prepared is really only in a position to react to events, rather than lead them. As this lack of preparation becomes apparent, the other negotiator will naturally feel strengthened in their position. They will, therefore, become more confident and resolute particularly if it is to prepare properly.

A negotiator must avoid using preparation time to rehearse a dogmatic defence of any given position, however deeply held, or to adopt an aggressive approach to the other negotiator's position. Constructive preparation is vital.

Defining Your Wants

You will negotiate to get what you want. In the preparation phase, you will decide or confirm what you want. Hence, the question you should ask yourself is: What do I want to happen as a result of this negotiation? The answer will be a list of your wants.

Merely quantifying what you want is obviously not an automatic guarantee that you are going to get it. In the course of the negotiation, you will have to modify your own wants, to a greater or lesser extent, to take account of the competing wants of the other negotiator.

It is also worth noting that opening negotiations may involve the reopening of previously settled issues: in the course of the negotiation for an overall advantage, it is possible to lose some issues which hitherto may have been taken for granted.

Mutual Objectives

In pursuing your own objectives through negotiation you must, of course, give consideration to the other party's objectives and their approach in attaining them. Establishing the other party's wants and gauging their priorities can be difficult. Particularly so, as it may be in their interests to conceal any such priorities and convince you that their demands are all of equal importance. You cannot baulk at such 'bluffing' ploys, if you yourself are inclined to take this approach. The other party's wants are obviously of importance, but they are only really of significance insofar as they influence the attainment of your own objectives.

Through negotiation, you might get what you want on their terms, or they might get what they want on your terms, or both of you might get some of your wants on each other's terms.

DISCUSSION

An important aim for any negotiator should be the extent to which they see their interactions as a mission to improve, or to impose. In a discussion, the parties present 'points of view', but are potentially open to learning from alternate perspectives that may result in an improved position or solution. There are no winners and losers in a discussion.

Debates, on the other hand, are marked by an adversarial approach, where each party comes equipped to promote their position and to undermine that of the other side. Indeed, debates are marked by 'sides'—in much the same way as we often depict negotiations—and are not designed to generate value-added outcomes.

These distinct approaches represent the difference between collaborative and adversarial negotiation. Most negotiators say they prefer collaborative, win-win negotiations. Most negotiation planning bears the hallmark of debate rather than discussion; a pre-planned justification for a fixed position, which the two parties will then justify through exaggeration and selective use of facts and which is maintained regardless of what others say.

Negotiators need to reflect on these questions. Are they discussing or debating? Is the approach they are taking appropriate to the goals they actually want to achieve? To what extent is their negotiating style reducing the possibility of an outcome? During this stage, individuals or members of each side put forward the case as they see it, that is, their understanding of the situation. Key skills during this stage include questioning, listening and clarifying.

CLARIFICATION OF GOALS

From the discussion, the goals, interests and viewpoints of both sides need to be clarified. For a negotiation to succeed, you need a clear sense of what you want the outcome to be. If you don't have defined goals in mind, you're unlikely to come away from negotiations with the outcome that's best for your business. Entering a negotiation with specific goals and a clear understanding of your next best alternative puts you in a stronger position.

It is helpful to list these factors in order of priority. Through this clarification it is often possible to identify or establish some common ground. Clarification is an essential part of the negotiation process; without it misunderstandings are likely to occur which may cause problems and barriers in reaching a beneficial outcome.

NEGOTIATING TOWARDS A WIN-WIN OUTCOME

This stage focuses on what is termed a 'win-win' outcome where both sides feel they have gained something positive through the process of negotiation and both sides feel their point of view has been taken into consideration.

The Real Win-Win Negotiation Concept

The true meaning of a win-win negotiated settlement is that the agreement reached cannot be improved further by any discussion. So your outcome cannot be improved for your benefit, and similarly, the agreement for the other party cannot be improved further for their benefit either. By definition, there is no value left on the table and all creative options have been thoroughly explored and exploited.

What does not constitute a win-win negotiation deal? We need to appreciate that not every agreement leads to a win-win scenario or outcome. In reality, very few negotiations reach this aspirational and theoretical ideal. Attitudes, positions and skills set invisible boundaries that constrain what we see as possible. Win-win deals are more likely when set up correctly through effective use of framing, research and building relationships at the right levels. If a win-win approach is appropriate, it's essential that we remember to pursue a win-win agreement for both parties.

A win-win outcome is usually the best result. Although this may not always be possible, through negotiation, it should be the ultimate goal. Suggestions of alternative strategies and compromises need to be considered at this point. Compromises are usually positive alternatives which can often achieve greater benefit for all concerned compared to holding to the original positions.

AGREEMENT

Agreement can be achieved when the understanding of both sides' viewpoints and interests have been considered. It is essential for everybody involved to keep an open mind in order to achieve an acceptable solution. Any agreement needs to be made perfectly clear so that both sides know what has been decided.

BATNA: Best Alternative To A Negotiated Agreement

BATNA is the most advantageous alternate course of action a party can take if negotiations fail and an agreement cannot be reached. BATNA is the key focus and driving force behind a successful negotiator. A party should generally not accept a worse resolution than its BATNA. Care should be taken, however, to ensure that deals are accurately valued, taking into account all considerations, such as relationship value, time value of money and the likelihood that the other party will live up to their side of the bargain. These are often difficult to value, since they are frequently based on uncertain or qualitative considerations, rather than easily measurable and quantifiable factors. The BATNA is often seen by negotiators not as a safety net, but rather as a point of leverage in negotiations. Attractive alternatives are needed to develop a strong BATNA.

IMPLEMENTING A COURSE OF ACTION

After the agreement, a course of action has to be implemented to execute the decision. The process is: Preparation → Action → Getting Started. Be alert for signs of readiness to take action. Mere vocal fervour about change is not necessarily a sign of determination to change. There may be decreased resistance. One party stops arguing, interrupting, denying or objecting. There are fewer questions about the problem. The said party seems to have enough information about the problem and stops asking questions. The party appears to have reached a resolution and may be more peaceful, calm, relaxed, unburdened or settled. Sometimes this happens after the party has passed through a period of anguish. The party makes direct self-motivational statements reflecting openness to change ('I have to do something.') and optimism ('I'm going to beat this.'). More questions about change come up. The client begins to talk about how life might be after a change, to anticipate difficulties if a change were made, or to discuss the advantages of change. If the client has had time between sessions, he may have begun experimenting with possible change approaches.

NEGOTIATING A PLAN FOR CHANGE

Creating a plan for change is the final step in readying your client to act. A solid plan for change enhances your client's self-efficacy and provides an opportunity to consider potential obstacles and the likely outcomes of each change strategy before embarking on to a final negotiation. Furthermore, nothing is more motivating than being well prepared—no matter what the situation, a well-prepared person is usually eager to get started.

2

Phases Of Negotiation

Negotiation is a method by which people settle differences. It is a process by which a compromise or an agreement is reached, while avoiding arguments and disputes. In any disagreement, individuals understandably aim to achieve the best possible outcome for their position (or perhaps an organisation they represent). However, the principles of fairness, seeking mutual benefit and maintaining a relationship are the keys to a successful outcome.

Specific forms of negotiation are used in different situations: international affairs, legal system, government, industrial disputes or domestic relationships. However, general negotiation skills can be learned and applied in a wide range of activities. Negotiation skills can be of great benefit in resolving any differences that arise between you and others.

Phases Of Negotiation

Prepare—What do you want?
• Decide what you want and prioritise (value) your wants.
Debate—What does the other party want?

• Disclose what you want but not the terms on which you might settle.
• Ask open questions and listen to the answers.
• Note the signals, which indicate willingness to consider alternatives.
Propose — What could you trade?
• Use 'If...then...' language. (If they meet some of your wants, then you might consider meeting some of their wants.)
• Keep quiet and wait for a response.
• Do not interrupt proposals.
Bargain—What will you trade?
• Trade the wants to agree to specific solutions.
• Be always conditional: 'if...then'
• Record what has been agreed.

Points to remember

- All negotiations have a common structure.
- Negotiators are always in one or other of the four phases common to all negotiations.
- Identify the phase you are in; this will help you to move the negotiation forward.

Diversions And Interruptions

Negotiations are often messy, involve many diversions and interruptions, and do not always move forward in a tidy fashion. Fortunately, however, this does not weaken the four-phase approach because it was from the real world of negotiating, with all its complexities, that the original analysis identified the phases and the sub-steps that link them.

Flexibility Of The Phases

It is perfectly acceptable to go backwards and forward between the phases. For example, while some preparation is completed before the first face-to-face meeting, additional preparation might be necessary because of what you discover once you meet the other negotiators. While debate may be a prelude to a proposal, the proposal may lead to more debate—before you get to another proposal! And so it goes on. For example, asking a question about a proposal or a bargain returns you to the debate phase.

It is possible to start with debate to learn what is wanted and then to adjourn to prepare your response. Some negotiations begin with proposals and then go on to a debate. When a question is asked to clarify a bargain, we are back in debate. During negotiations, we might return to preparation several times. For each phase of negotiation, there are techniques that work and others that do not.

All negotiations involve varying combinations. Knowing which phase you are in, enables you to adapt your own behaviour to the circumstances. For each phase, there are certain techniques that work and others that do not.

Manage Your Negotiation

Instead of relying on nothing more than an instinctive reaction to the other negotiator, you are able to choose how to respond. You know what phase you are in, what actions or reactions on your part will help the phase to move forward and what will hinder progress. You are no longer guessing what to do next in your negotiations because you are able to manage what you are doing.

Whether your opponent is aware of the phases or not, makes little difference. If they are aware of them, this will assist both of you to move competently towards a settlement, if one is possible. If they are not aware of the phases, their reactions may be comparatively disorganised or badly managed, but yours will not be and this will give you a negotiating edge.

A proposal is a proposal in any language. Their proposals may be poorly phrased, unconditional or just a one-way demand. Yours will always be conditional. The difference will help to educate them in how to do business: nobody gets what they want unless and until you get offered some of what you want.

One party may be stuck in an argument, while you prefer to explore each other's wants in a constructive debate. Your understanding of the role of each phase assists your attempts to find a solution. Whether they anxiously work through a phase or stumble through it makes little difference to you. Your approach is a conscious application of effective behaviour in each phase. You—and they—will notice the difference.

What Is The Negotiation About?

All negotiations take place in a context, which influences the negotiators' behaviours and their aspirations, the types of issues that are addressed and the range of possible outcomes.

Issues That Have To Be Addressed

An issue is anything over which the negotiators have discretion. For example, issues could include the price of a product, the quantity available, where a country's boundary line runs, how flexible a contract clause must be and so on. Through negotiation, issues lead to the decisions of the parties involved.

What Do You Want?

Wants are preferences in respect of the issues. They are the decisions you prefer to arrive at, though what you want may have to be modified as a result of accommodating the other negotiator's wants. For example: I may want to pay a lower price for your business because of the uncertainty about future profits, while you may want a higher price because you wish to retire in a state of affluence. Through negotiation, we might be able to find a way to meet both our wants (e.g. a purchase price paid in two branches, one on my acquiring the business, which meets my concerns, the other when its true profits are proven, which meet your ambitions).

List And Prioritise Wants

- For every issue, you should write down what you want.
- You can be as vague or specific as you want and for the moment you need not concern yourself with what the other negotiator might want.

- Now assess how important each of these wants is to you. In short, prioritise your wants. Some wants will be more important than others, some wants you may not be sure about just yet. You may use any categories of importance that you find convenient, such as high, medium and low.

> **High importance:** These are those objectives that you must get if you are to agree at all. These represent the 'bottom line' or 'limit position'. They are the ones without which a negotiator is not prepared to reach any agreement.

> **Medium importance:** These are those objectives that you would prefer to attain if you could, but which are not critical.

> **Low importance:** These are those objectives that you would like to attain if you could, but would not let them jeopardise the deal.

Evaluate Wants

Next you must assign ranges of possible values to each of the issues you have prioritised. This requirement is based on the notion that negotiators do not enter the negotiations exactly where they intend to settle—if they did this would imply that there was no movement possible and the negotiation would degenerate into a battle of wills or a power struggle. Negotiating from fixed and inflexible positions is extremely difficult. Despite being easily avoidable, it remains the most common cause of deadlock between negotiators. Giving yourself a range gives you flexibility as well as a greater chance of reaching an agreement.

Entry And Exit Positions

Hence, you will tend to enter the negotiation with statements of requirements on the issues which you certainly know, and the other negotiator almost certainly will assume, will not be your final position. They will know that wherever you start from, you are probably willing to move somewhat further. The range, therefore, will begin with an 'entry' position and end with an 'exit' position. This also provides the rationale for never accepting a negotiator's first offer—because wherever they open there is another position, better for you, where they will go before they close.

Where To Enter And Where To Exit

Where you enter will depend on the circumstances and on what you believe you can credibly defend for the other negotiator. Unrealistic or overly ambitious objectives should be abandoned prior to the negotiations as putting them forward could antagonise the other negotiator into similarly unrealistic demands. Where you exit will also depend on the circumstances and on what options you have in case you cannot reach an agreement.

If you are sure you have many alternate options, your entry point might be relatively ambitious and your exit point relatively close to where you began. If you are not so sure of your strengths, or are convinced that you have few options (few customers, few opportunities), you are likely to enter relatively 'softly' and be prepared to exit even more 'softly' if you have to. Nevertheless, it is a common failing of diffident negotiators to err on the side of caution, aiming lower rather than higher.

Record Preparation Details

The details of your preparation can be recorded on a single sheet of paper. The detail you wish to go into will depend on the importance of the negotiations. No matter how short your time, some consideration of the issues to be decided will automatically improve your negotiation performance. It is important to know what you want from the negotiation.

Relative importance attached to your wants:

- How you would present your wants, in the form of a range from your entry position to your exit position.
- Effective handling of face-to-face interaction, the debate phase, will do much to consolidate the advantages gained from improved preparation.

How To Prepare

A manufacturer uses a specialised machine tool for making some high-quality components. A problem has emerged with the availability of the machine tool due to some recurring maintenance fault, delays in the supplier's technicians arriving to correct the fault, and errors on the part of the operators.

The manufacturer has arranged a meeting with the supplier to resolve the problem. It is anticipated that the meeting will lead to negotiation. Independent of this situation, the supplier had already approached the manufacturer with a request to increase prices on the grounds that the maintenance contract was unprofitable.

What might the manufacturer's negotiator do in preparation for the meeting? Apart from collecting recent data on the machine's unavailability and the reasons for each incident, the negotiator would begin to assess the question: What do we want?

Checklist For Preparation

- What do you want as a result of this negotiation?
- What are the negotiable issues?
- What do you want for each issue?
- Rank each want by its importance to you.

  High—absolutely critical—certain no deal

  Medium—important but not critical

  Low—would like to achieve but shall not sacrifice the deal if not obtained

- What are your entry and exit limits?
- Entry terms should be credible.
- Exit terms are your 'walking away' positions.
- All prepared positions are subject to revision if circumstances suggest changes are advisable.

Common Mistakes:

- Not finding time to decide what you want
- Confusing 'let's hear what they have to say' with preparation
- Being unrealistic when deciding on your entry and exit points
- Not prioritising your wants
- Not setting a range for each want

PHASE II

How To Debate

Debate is the most common form of interaction between negotiators. It accounts for an estimated 80 per cent of time spent in negotiations.

This makes debate a key area for self-improvement because by your conduct in debate with other negotiators, you can slow down, hinder, deadlock or alternatively promote a settlement. This is because you can control two things during debates: how you present yourself and how you react to the other negotiator (no matter how they are behaving).

Your approach to debate will influence the progress and outcome of the negotiation. This will not just be at a particular stage either, as the debate phase will continue throughout the negotiation.

Coping with debate, getting it to work in favour of your negotiation on objectives and not against them, will significantly improve your performance as a negotiator.

Using Debate To Gauge The Other Negotiator's Views

Preparation will have clarified your own standpoint on the issues. You now have to gauge the other negotiator's views. Preparation will also have included conjecture on your part, which you will now have the opportunity to test.

The other negotiator will usually need little encouragement to disclose their opinions. They will represent their entry position and all successive 'current' positions as their exit position as far as you are concerned.

The more you can find out about their position—by questioning and clarification—the more information you can gain about their commitment to their position and the direction in which they may be prepared to move.

Debate provides a crucial opportunity to gain information about the other negotiator's objectives and attitudes. In this way, you can gauge their commitment and identify their interests and intentions; equally important, you will discover their inhibitions. An interest will encourage someone to say 'Yes', an inhibition will encourage them to say 'No'. Neither factor will be immediately obvious to you and you will initially be reliant upon assumptions. Debate will, therefore, give you the opportunity to test these assumptions. Foreknowledge of another party's plans, wants or objectives will also offer you the chance to test their candour or basic honesty.

Effective use of debating time should allow you to explore the other's inhibitions as well as your own. Creating this open dialogue between both parties will probably have one of the two consequences. It will either lead to an acknowledgement of the mutual benefits of negotiating a settlement or it will demonstrate that a settlement is neither possible nor desirable.

If you concentrate on debate—to find out what the other negotiator wants and let them know what you want—you will avoid disruptive diversions and destructive arguments.

Destructive Argument

Destructive argument is a temptation in this phase because it helps prevent too close an examination of opening positions. It is an all-too-common feature of many negotiations and is most likely to arise where parties are highly committed, anxious or angry. A prime example would be the practice of interrupting. A simple, yet fundamental, step that you can take to improve your performance in negotiations is to avoid interrupting other people.

Other features of destructive argument to be avoided include:

- regularly point-scoring on issues.
- attacking or blaming somebody for a problem.
- sarcasm and other forms of disrespect.
- personal insults.
- ascribing ulterior motives to other people.
- not listening to what others are saying.
- reacting to provocation.

Consequences Of Destructive Argument

Few people can resist point-scoring—reminding the other party of their past failures.

The blame- and attack/defence cycles are well-established elements of destructive arguments. When someone is attacked, they will instinctively defend themselves, however irrelevant the attack is to the main objectives of the negotiation. Attempts to apportion blame will either provoke spontaneous resistance or efforts to retaliate by passing the blame back to you.

As an attack/defence cycle proceeds, there are personal attacks, emotional tension and interpersonal relationships suffer damage as a result.

Negotiators' inhibitions, including their fears and concerns about your intentions, are reinforced by destructive arguments. Inhibitions hinder negotiation and can even be a set-back to an agreement which is mutually advantageous.

Some people are wholly concerned with winning any movement. The result of such behaviour can only be to drive the negotiators apart.

Reduce Tension

Negotiations often begin with a degree of tension. This can be because of the history of the relationship, warring nations, poor industrial relations, failure to perform past or current contracts, squabbling relatives, etc. It can also be because the negotiators do not know each other or are uncertain of what is about to be decided. If tension is present, preventing it from worsening into outright hostility is imperative.

Negotiators can do a lot to reduce tension by what they say and how they speak to each other. You can help reduce tension, if you remember that your sole task in debate is basically to assess what the other negotiator wants and to inform them of what you want.

Establish Rapport

You can begin by establishing a rapport with the other negotiator. Rapport establishes your relationship. This sets the tone of the relationship in the first few minutes. Your tone can work against you, if you appear hostile (because you feel angry). You can also undermine your negotiating position by too subservient a tone in which you are so desperate to be friendly that you give up your own wants.

Therefore:

- show and earn respect.
- follow set norms of greeting and non-business talk.

Determine The Order Of Business

Next, set an agenda for the meeting. This can be done formally in writing or informally with a verbal summary of what you propose to discuss. Always invite amendments and comments on the subjects and their order.

Describe what you are seeking

In describing the broad conclusions you are seeking, reassure the other negotiator(s) by using tactful and non-threatening terms.

You must explain your ideal position before you can expect the other negotiators to move towards it. Each party must know the other's ideal position in order to assess its proximity to their own limit.

Avoid threats

Do not state or imply a threat in your opening remarks.

For example: 'If we cannot reach a sensible settlement here, we may have to consider litigation.'

Threats are certain to provoke resentment. Your opposite number does not need to be reminded of the consequences of failure before you start. Threats produce either counter-threats or statements of defiance and are thus likely to lead to argument before negotiations have even begun.

Listen Positively

To find out what the other party wants, listen to what they say (the more they talk—and the less you do—at this stage, the better). Ask them questions about what they want and listen to their answers. Anyone who tells you what they want in negotiation is doing you a favour—so if they launch into a monologue, you should listen for clues as to their wants and not interrupt.

You must support positive listening behaviour with positive talking behaviour—making sure you use the time effectively. One way to do this is to ask open questions which encourage explanation and elaboration by the other negotiator.

Use Questions

Questions are both under-rated and badly used negotiating tools. Below average negotiators do not ask enough, if any, questions and many negotiators who do ask questions ask the wrong kind in the wrong tone.

Keep the doors open, if you want to be an effective negotiator. Never say 'No', instead ask an open question: 'If we were to agree to your proposal, what would you be willing to offer in return?' Open questions unlock doors.

Don't disagree—ask your opponent an open question instead. When a negotiator makes a statement that you disagree with, you will achieve little if you tell them they are wrong. While you are explaining why they are wrong, they will be thinking of how to defend themselves, perhaps by raising irrelevant matters, perhaps by attacking you. It is much more effective for you to ask open questions about the basis for the statement that you disagree with and for them either to show their statement to be true (in which case you can change your own position without loss of face), or to show that their own statement is false (in which case they can retract without feeling aggrieved).

Right And Wrong Questions To Ask

Examples of the wrong types of question to ask include:

- Are you listening?
- Are you serious?
- Do you think I am stupid?
- Is that your final offer?

These are tension-inducing questions that are likely to lead you away from an early settlement, perhaps into an irretrievable deadlock.

Examples of the right type of questions include:

- What criterion are you using?
- What are your priorities?
- How do you calculate those numbers?

These questions seek information using an open question format which normally requires an extended answer, rather than a simple 'Yes' or 'No'. By using words like 'what', 'why', 'when', 'how', 'where', and 'who', you invite the other negotiators to explain themselves and to disclose their wants.

When asking open questions, it is essential to make considered use of language. 'How did you arrive at that conclusion?' should elicit useful details about the other negotiator's reasoning. 'Do you think I am stupid?', on the other hand, which you might be equally tempted to say, would provoke a counter-productive emotional defence, telling you nothing.

Summarising

Before you make any response, it is a good idea to summarise what they have proposed. You can either ask them to do it, or alternatively do it yourself, highlighting any implications and their (not your) attitude towards them. This has many uses.

- Simplifies complex issues
- Helps refocus wandering negotiations

- Reassures that they are being taken seriously
- Gives you time to think

Arguments, Principles And Opinions Cannot Be Negotiated

We can only negotiate proposals and therefore debate is more effective if it informs the negotiators of what each wants, because their proposals will have to address those wants. We cannot negotiate the 'truth' or 'falsity' of someone's beliefs, values, principles or opinions. These lead only to argument.

Movement

Parties to a negotiation must move from their current preferred solution to some other acceptable solution if an agreement is to be reached. The negotiator's problem is how to make this happen—how to ensure that movement by one side is reciprocated by movement by the other side. The principal motivations for moving are incentives (benefits of agreeing) and sanctions (penalties for not agreeing). These forces may be explicit (attention being drawn to the consequences of agreeing or disagreeing) or implied.

Negotiation is motivated by self-interest. People negotiate because the other party offers them an incentive or threatens them with a sanction. Without either of these, there is no negotiation. If you are satisfied with the status quo — have nothing to trade and want nothing on offer — you will not negotiate.

However committed the parties appear to be to their position, and however unwilling to trade, they would not be involved in negotiating if they were not willing to consider moving towards an agreement.

Deadlock

A deadlock can occur when both parties rely on the strategy of sticking to their current position until the other is willing to move. If both sides adopt this approach, there will be no movement.

Why should a party be unwilling to negotiate? Distrust and tension may be present. One party may see its interests as being best served by resisting change of any kind and maintaining the existing situation. Only if they come to believe that the potential outcome is likely to be an improvement in the existing situation or less damaging than the possible consequences of the existing situation, will they be willing to negotiate.

Why Else Is Compromise Avoided?

Movement can be interpreted as weakness. If you refuse to move for long enough, the other party may ultimately 'surrender'; alternatively the negotiation may fail completely.

Inexperienced negotiators often fall into the trap of giving a 'No' too soon, resulting in an unsatisfactory agreement, or no movement at all, thereby achieving no agreement.

Balancing Firmness And Flexibility

There is a dilemma faced by all negotiators: how do you suggest flexibility in your entry requirements without giving in? Once you move from a position, there is a danger that one move will be led by another, until you have nothing left to negotiate and nothing to show for your movement. Below-average negotiators do not move at all. They try intimidation, with the intention of forcing the other negotiator to give in, or in the hope that they will do so. Effective negotiators, however, listen and watch for signals.

Looking For Signals

Every negotiation has at least two solutions to the same issue — the solution that meets your wants and the solution that meets the other party's wants. Your strategic task is to arrive at an agreed solution, which almost certainly will be different from either of the two solutions with which the negotiation began. Hence, you look for signals or signs of a willingness to consider movement.

Signalling behaviour can be used to handle movement confidently.

A signal is a means by which parties indicate their willingness to negotiate on something. It implies willingness only if it is reciprocated by the other side and not treated as a first step on the slippery slope to surrender.

Advantages Of Signalling Behaviour

- Can be used to break the cycle of circular argument
- Allows you to make new proposals without being seen to be giving in
- Familiar behaviour we often use — nothing new to learn

What Are Signals?

Signals are qualifications attached to a statement. For example:

- Our normal price is… (But we have a different price for special circumstances.)
- It would be extremely difficult… (But not necessarily impossible.)
- We do not want to be locked into this deal… (We need an escape clause.)

The negotiator suggests the possibility of agreement if the other party's proposal is amended in some way. It is an invitation to the other party to move. It says that although the present proposal is unacceptable, it would be negotiable if put in another form.

Responding To Signals

Signals hint at the possibilities of movement if, and only if, the other negotiator responds positively. At this stage, the category of response is crucial. Of course, if the other negotiator attacks the signaller, you can be sure that they will slip back towards argument.

- I don't care about your normal prices.
- So after an hour of pretending it was impossible to change the contract, you now agree it can be changed.
- You are either in the deal totally or there is no deal at all.

Summarise Signals

The most effective way to respond to a signal is to confirm what you heard by summarising what is said to you—even if you do not yet see how the signal helps you—and then encourage the other party to expand on theirs.

- Under what circumstances would you consider a non-list price?

- How could we make it easier for you to re-examine this clause?

- How can we address your concerns about being locked in?

This type of open questions can reveal their wants in greater detail and what wants of yours they might be prepared to meet.

Signalling does not inevitably lead to an agreement nor resolve conflict. It makes negotiation about the issues possible and leads to the possibility of an agreement. Signals lead to proposals—they are the bridge between debate and attempts to trade.

Adjourn

Wherever possible, you should take an adjournment at this point to consider what you have learned about the other negotiator's wants and to assess the initial reactions to the statement of your own wants. In short, you should return to the preparation phase to plan your movement to the proposal phase. Taking a short break is not as difficult as it might seem. Very few negotiations over major issues are settled in a single meeting and using a natural break—in those that are—is not beyond most negotiators to suggest or arrange.

CHECKLIST FOR SIGNALLING

- Are there signs of potential movement in the debate?

- What signals have you given to indicate your willingness to consider moving?

- If they have been ignored, how might you reword them?

- What is the cause of the other party's 'stonewalling'? Confidence, or lack of it?

- Test 'stonewalling' by a specific signal linked to a direct call for them to reciprocate.

- If there is still no response, you can:
  - suspend the negotiation.
  - require them to seek authority to revise their position.

- Avoid making unilateral concessions in the hope that they will respond because this only rewards their intransigence.

- Listen for their use of non-absolute and qualified statements of their position or references to their inhibitions.

- Respond positively, but vaguely. For example: I am always prepared to consider constructive suggestions for improving the acceptability of my proposals.

Remember:

- Ignoring signals prolongs debate.
- Listen more; talk less.
- Respond and reciprocate positively.
- Reward signals not intransigence.

Common Mistakes:

- Ignoring signals
- Moving in response to intransigence
- Not exploring the implications of a signal
- Not reacting positively to a signal

CHECKLIST FOR DEBATE

Differing Entry and Exit Points

Avoid:

- Mocking
- Interrupting
- Point-scoring
- Attacking
- Blaming
- Talking too much
- Shouting them down
- Sarcasm
- Threatening

Practise:

- listening.

- asking questions for clarification.

- summarising issues neutrally (and briefly).

- asking them to justify their case on an item-by-item base (watch for signals).

- being non-committal about their explanations.

- looking for clues about their priorities and testing their commitment to their positions.

- seeking and giving information.

Common Mistakes:

- Asking closed questions

- Not listening

- Arguing to 'win'

- Not summarising

- Making mountains out of molehills

PHASE III

How To Propose

You will be ready to propose when you are able to summarise what the other negotiator wants and when you have informed the other negotiator of what you want. In your preparation, you identified the issues and what you wanted. You must think about what the other negotiator wants and, if possible, their order of priorities.

Wants

Competing wants

In stating their wants, they are likely to have revealed their entry positions. This gives you crucial information. By comparing their wants with yours and the respective entry points, you can see at a glance what wants, if any, you have in common, which of your respective wants are in direct competition with each other and which individual wants are not contested by either of you.

Proposal language

Your opponent's initial proposal will be a statement of their ideal position. You can judge the flexibility of their position by the language used: 'I must insist on…', 'I was hoping for…'

Wants normally have different entry points and the question is whether or not there is an overlap in your exit points. For example, if what the buyer will pay is less than (i.e. does not overlap with) the least the seller will accept, they are unlikely to reach an agreement unless one or both change their exit points. The fact that their entry points are different is not important—we expect negotiators to enter some distance from where they intend to settle.

Competing and compatible wants

Competitive wants often dominate negotiations. You want a higher price, the buyer wants a lower price; you prefer to limit your liability, the buyer prefers that you accept consequential loss.

Compatible wants are those where it is in your common interest to agree—you both want a workable safety policy that enables you to protect your employees.

The existence of compatible wants can help reconcile differences in the competing wants. By trading movement between the wants, we can avoid a competitive deadlock, particularly where the negotiators signal agreement in the compatible want of high priority.

New issues emerge in debate

New issues, emerging through the medium of debate, can be those which you have not so far considered or which are only of interest to the other party. The latter are the most useful; relatively unimportant to you, but essential to them. These wants can be invaluable in subsequent proposing and bargaining and it is vital not to concede them unilaterally. They can form the crucial item in our trade in wants.

What is a proposal?

A proposal is a tentative answer to the question: Which wants of the other negotiator might I have to meet if I am to get what I want? Therefore, a proposal is more effective if it is conditional: 'If you give me some of my wants, then I could give you some of your wants.' It conveys the tentative terms upon which you might do business.

The two elements of a proposal

A proposal consists of two elements: the condition and the offer. The condition states what you want from the other negotiator and the offer states what you might trade in return.

Make proposals conditional

Proposals are more effective when they are conditional: 'If you consider my concerns, then I will consider your concerns.'

A tentative conditional proposal will give you an advantage by leaving you room to manoeuvre in later stages of the negotiating process. If you concede while proposing, bargaining will be much more difficult.

Condition only: Such a proposal consists only of a condition and demands that the other negotiators give in. Statement like 'You will pay in advance' could cause offence by their abruptness and apparent lack of an offer of anything in return.

Offer only: A proposal consisting only of an offer is a unilateral concession to the other party's demands. 'We will give you a discount of 15 per cent' might result in the other side's goodwill, but is more likely to provoke further demands. If you will give 15 per cent for nothing, what else will you concede under real pressure?

Vague or specific: Your condition may be vague or specific, but your offer must always be vague, though expressed firmly.

- If you could improve your delivery schedules, then I could consider minimum volume orders.
- If you could improve your delivery schedules by three days, then I could consider minimum volume orders.

Why should proposed offers always be an issue?

Why? Because for as long as it is not clear—what proposal will be acceptable—it is necessary to have some flexibility.

The vagueness of the offer does precisely that—it leaves you room for movement without giving in. You offer to 'consider/ look at/rethink' the acceptability of the other party's wants, or you might offer to 'find a way to do something about' this or that want.

Degree of flexibility

Flexibility is the extent to which you are prepared to move from your initial position. Too little flexibility could give the impression that you are unwilling to negotiate at all, causing the other party to abandon negotiations. Alternatively, too much will signal that you are not committed to your position and you will not be taken seriously. The answer is to retain sufficient flexibility to revise your position upwards or downwards, when necessary.

How To Make A Proposal

State what your proposal is. Then stop talking. Make sure you do not interrupt the silence—you could end up making unnecessary concessions or diverting attention from your proposal to your explanations. Silence will put the other negotiator under pressure. You have seized the initiative— it's up to them to justify their contention that your proposal is unacceptable.

Either/Or proposal

This is a variation which has certain advantages. By giving the other party a choice between proposals you reduce the likelihood that they will instantly accept or reject and by the choices they make, you will gain further insight into their position.

Responding To A Proposal

You do not expect a 'Yes' to a proposal, although even if you do get a 'Yes', there is still a lot of work to do. You will then be required to specify the actual content of your hitherto vague offer. An affirmative reply to your proposal only suggests that the other party is at least interested in exploring the exchange you have suggested.

Use questions to respond to a proposal

Questions are the most effective response to a conditional proposal, either to question the condition, to uncover details of the vague offer, clarifying any ambiguities or aspects that are not understood.

- For a discount, I would require a substantial increase in volume.
- What volume do you have in mind?

Summarise the proposal

Whether you find the proposal acceptable or not, attempt to summarise it. You need not be concerned that merely talking about the proposal makes it acceptable because nothing is agreed until you say it is 'agreed'.

Beware of saying 'No'

The most common mistake people make is to say 'No' to anything with which they disagree. Not that you should never say 'No'—there are circumstances when 'No' is sufficient—but an instant negative is often counter-productive. They perhaps did not give their proposal sufficient attention (remember the need for mutual respect). Moreover, an instant 'No' gives insufficient information to discriminate between the absolute 'No', in the sense of 'Never', and the relative 'No', in the sense of 'maybe, if there were some changes'.

Don't respond instantly

In fact, any instant response—whether a negative or a counter-proposal—is likely to send the wrong signal, that is, that you are only interested in your own solution and not the other negotiator's contribution.

How to receive a proposal: A summary

Don't interrupt: A free concession often comes at the end of a statement and will be missed out; you might also cause antagonism. Don't instantly reject a proposal.

Considered Alternative Proposal

A considered alternative proposal is a considered response to the proposed exchange of wants suggested by the other negotiator. It follows consideration of what has been proposed and exploration, by questioning and listening, of the content of their proposal. It is a considered alternative rather than a direct and confrontational counter-proposal because it embodies, where possible, elements of the other negotiator's proposals into your own suggested solution.

Your considered alternative proposal

By questioning a proposal for a 15 per cent volume discount for an unspecified increase in the order, it is revealed that they are considering 'perhaps doubling' the order. While the principle of a volume discount is acceptable, your concern may be that you could discount your prices and then find that the increased order does not materialise and, moreover, you might consider that a 15 per cent discount is too high. Having considered the proposal and made a judgement about its worth to you, you could make a considered alternative proposal, such as, 'If you contract to take 150 per cent more volume over the next twelve months, then I would be willing to consider a retrospective volume discount of 10 per cent.'

The other negotiator's considered alternate response

Perhaps you are willing to reduce the qualifying volume below 150 per cent, to raise the discount above 10 per cent, and to amend the retrospective condition. That would be for them to explore and to make a considered alternative proposal to you, such as, 'If you make a 10 per cent discount on current invoices up to when I reach last year's order levels, and then 15 per cent on all orders from then on, then I am prepared to accept the final 15 per cent discount retrospectively.'

Middle Ground

Somewhere between the two converging considered alternative proposals, there is a settlement waiting to be discovered.

In general, you trade things of less value to you than to them, in exchange for things of less value to them than to you. For example, when you are thirsty you exchange money for a drink. You value the money at that moment less than you do the means to quench your thirst. If you did not, you would keep your money and forgo the drink; the person with the drink values your money more than they value the drink. If they did not, they would keep their drink and forgo your money. The basis of trade is to exchange the money for the drink, or the drink for the money, with both parties gaining by getting what they want from the transaction.

CHECKLIST FOR PROPOSING

- Proposals are more productive than arguments because arguments cannot be negotiated.
- Proposals can advance negotiations.
- Proposals can seize the initiative.
- Unrealistic proposals divide the negotiators.
- Interrupting proposals provokes arguments.
- Proposals must address the wants of the parties.
- Proposals can be used to initiate responses.
- Be firm on generalities—For example: 'We must have compensation.'
- Be flexible on specifics—For example: 'We suggest ₹1 lakh compensation.'
- Do not use unassertive language. For example: 'We hope...', 'We like...' and 'We prefer...'.
- Use strong language. For example: 'We need...', 'We must have...' and 'We require...'
- State your conditions first and be vague or specific.
- Follow with your offer and be tentative.

Remember:
- Don't just complain; propose a remedy.
- Open realistically.

- Move in small steps.
- Invite a response.

Common Mistakes:

- Complaining but not proposing
- Using unassertive language—For example: 'I'd like...' and 'We wish...'
- Making unconditional offers
- Negotiating with yourself before you meet the other side
- Opening with an unrealistic condition or offer
- Behaving inconsistently in moving your position
- Interrupting a proposal
- Assuming the other negotiator's proposal to be set in stone instead of being open to negotiation

PHASE IV

Bargaining

Bargaining involves making exchanges—giving something up in return for gaining something else. It is the phase of negotiation which can make the difference between a successful and an unsuccessful outcome of the process—both parties must pay strict attention to what they are doing in order to avoid making untraded concessions.

There are a number of techniques a negotiator can use to ensure they reach an agreement favourable to their interests.

A bargain conveys the precise terms on which you would settle

A bargain is a specific solution to the negotiating problem: What agreement is acceptable to both of us? A bargain states the precise terms under which you propose to reach an agreement, either on a single issue or on all of the issues.

Bargains are always conditional: A fundamental principle of bargaining is to make any offers conditional. Nothing is ever given away for free—everything that is conceded must be traded for something else.

Approach To Bargaining

All bargains should be expressed in a common format.

If you...then I...

For example: 'If you agree to...I will agree to...'

The key words are 'If you agree to...' Without this provision the other negotiator could simply accept the offer without anything in return.

Similarly, the nature and scope of the trade-off that you suggest will signal the value that you attach to your offer. It will also show the other negotiator that you intend to concede nothing unless it is matched by a similar effort on their part. Without establishing this conditional approach, they may feel that they will have gained any concessions that you offer as of right, or via the apparent strength of their position.

'If...then...' pitfall

Not all the ways of saying 'If...then' are automatically helpful. For instance, saying: 'If we agree to your demand, then will you agree to ours?' Although this appears to use the 'If...then...' format, it is a question and not a statement. Bargains state the cost of agreement to the other party and do not merely ask a closed question that could invite a negative response or entail prolonged haggling.

Condition And Offer

Like a proposal, a bargain consists of a condition plus an offer. The condition will specify precisely what you want from the other negotiator, if you are to commit in your offer to any of the other negotiator's precise wants.

Unlike a proposal, a bargain consists of a precise condition and a precise offer. There is nothing vague about a bargain.

Using the approach we have discussed, a bargain takes the following form: 'If you agree to limit compensation for damages to ₹35,000, then we will issue a credit note for this amount on next year's business.'

Use condition and offer together

A condition on its own is an ultimatum and, as such, is likely to be treated less than favourably. Conversely, an offer on its own is a free gift and is likely to provoke a demand for more of the same. Only a conditional precise offer in the specific format of 'If you...then I...' can secure an agreement without giving in.

Always lead with conditions

When presenting a revised offer, you must not forget to match each further offer with an appropriate condition. Negotiators are sometimes so concerned with getting their revised offer right and putting it across to the other negotiator that they forget to place conditions upon it.

Any retrospective attempt to introduce such conditions will probably be treated with some suspicion by the other party. They will either be unwilling to take the condition seriously—after all, you have already made the offer—or they will regard it as a breach of convention—a 'moving of the goalposts'.

Therefore, you should always lead with your conditions. You are then in a position to bargain relative to your stated requirements.

A Bargain Is Specific If It Seeks Agreement

When you bargain, you are actively seeking agreement. A 'Yes' response to a bargain is a deal. If there is any vagueness about a bargain, it would be indistinguishable from a proposal. You can say 'Yes' to a bargain and end the negotiation on the offered conditional terms. By saying 'Yes', you are accepting both—the conditions and the offer.

'Yes' concludes the negotiation

When you bargain, there is no more ambiguity about what you would exchange for what you want. If they say 'Yes', the negotiation is concluded and apart from writing up the agreement there is nothing more to negotiate about in respect of the offered bargain.

Responding To A Bargain

Your response to a bargain depends on whether you accept or do not accept the offered deal without further negotiation.

Should you elect to accept it, you merely inform the other negotiator of your acceptance in whatever manner is culturally acceptable. Usually, saying 'agreed', or words to that effect, is enough.

Making a condition counter-bargain

If it is unacceptable in its current form, your best response is to propose a conditional counter-bargain containing your amended terms. Arguing is a weak response because it returns you to the midst of the debate phase and is unlikely to produce a revised bargain. You may, nevertheless, return to the debate phase to explore possibilities of movement— by asking further questions or looking for signals as to possible areas of renegotiation.

Using an instant counter-bargains

It is quite common for negotiators to propose counter-bargains that amend each other's last conditional offer, without a great deal of additional debate on the merits of their cases. Instant counter-bargains are acceptable in the bargaining phase and have much to accelerate the momentum of the negotiation towards its ultimate conclusion.

Exchange Of Proposals

An exchange of proposals could spark off a run at an attempted bargain. The ease with which negotiators slip from a proposal (vague conditional offer) to a bargain (specific conditional offer) often moves a negotiation to a close soon. By the time the negotiators are ready to bargain, they should have a fair knowledge of what is likely to be acceptable and how far they have to move to trade for what they want.

Approaches To Bargaining Problems

- If they do not accept your bargain, remember that arguing for or against a bargain is usually ineffective.

- If they reject your bargain, require them to propose their alternative.

- If you reject their bargain, try a counter-bargain that changes the conditions or the offer, or both, in your favour.

- Work towards an agreement.

Arguing is a common mistake

The most common mistake is to continue to argue against proposals that you disagree with. By argument alone, you miss the opportunity of using a considered alternative proposal—particularly one that incorporates by design the elements of the other negotiator's original proposal—to move into the bargaining phase.

Instead of disagreeing in the hope that they will change their mind on the basis of your arguments alone, you can move them from their current proposal by offering them a precise bargain. This could take the form of: 'If you drop/amend/change your conditions or offer (in the following way), then I will improve/alter or change my offer (in this way).'

Deadlock

Just as a proposal diffuses a deadlocked debate, so a bargain can unblock a deadlocked proposal.

Negotiating Several Issues

Where more than one issue is in contention (the normal case), it is important to abide by these two principles.

- Nothing is agreed until everything is agreed.
- All issues are linked together.

Keep the whole deal together.

The first principle effectively guarantees the second. A piece-meal agreement on an isolated issue could leave you short of negotiating room when you reach the later issues. Your problem then would be how to open out on the outstanding issues without giving in. On the other hand, by keeping the issues linked, you have the means to keep the negotiation open until all the issues are covered.

Nothing is agreed upon until everything is agreed

The significance of linking issues: This approach could be countered by the apparently logical suggestion that the list of demands, objections or requirements, etc., should be dealt with one at a time. For one thing, an item-by-item approach has administrative advantages, if only in the sense of an orderly agenda.

Nevertheless, you must on no account be persuaded that an administrative convenience implies that provisional agreement on issues in a list, shuts the door on all further consideration of the issues when there is deadlock on delayed issues. All the disputed and agreed issues should be linked together in the bargaining phase.

By negotiating each item individually, you could be forced to make concessions on each and every point. When you reach the stage of negotiating any issues that remain, you may find yourself having nothing left to bargain with.

At this point, you will be abandoning all hope of reaching an agreement and shouldering whatever costs this may entail; or seeking authorisation to improve your offer and taking the inevitable criticism from your colleagues.

CHECKLIST FOR BARGAINING

- Absolutely firm rule—no exceptions at all, ever. 'Every offer must be conditional.'
- Decide what you require in exchange for your offers.
- List and place that at the front of your proposal.
- Keep all the issues linked and trade off a move on one for a new condition or a move on something else.
- Be ready to bring back into contention any previously 'settled' issues, if you need negotiating room under pressure of deadlock on a point.

Remember:
- 'If you...then I...'
- Never give something for nothing.
- Lead with your conditions.
- Keep the issues linked.

Common Mistakes:

- Unconditional offers
- Asking permission to concede using question proposals: If I…will you…?
- Forgetting to state your conditions
- Separating the offer from the conditions with explanatory comments
- Agreeing to issues one at a time
- Not linking movement on one issue to movement on another

Bargaining Possibilities:

- They get what they want on your terms.
- You get what you want on their terms.
- You both get some of what you want on each other's terms.

PHASE V

Agreement

There are two major pressures which a negotiator has to contend with. The first of these stems from the fundamental uncertainty of negotiating: never really knowing whether you are anywhere near the other negotiator's exit limit. As a result, you delay coming to a decision about what is on offer at any moment just in case there is more you can get. The other pressure urges you to come to an agreement before the other negotiator has the opportunity to 'squeeze' you any further towards your exit limit.

The longer the negotiations continue, the more time you have to extract all the concessions available from them but, by the same token, the longer you negotiate the more time they have to do the same to you.

The Importance Of Closing Techniques

Inexperienced negotiators often find it difficult to know when, or how, to close deals. As a result, they frequently continue negotiations for too long and, in the process, risk conceding further, apparently 'minor', points. When taken as a whole, however, these could represent a substantial additional concession.

Terminating a negotiation is often difficult

You do not want to say 'Yes' in case you can improve on the other negotiator's current offer; you do not want to continue saying 'No' in case they come up with something you would rather keep out of the discussion. Hence, you dither.

Deciding when to close: It is easier to learn how to close than when to close. The decision to close the bargaining phase is a matter of judgement, as it is rare for both parties simultaneously to reach their respective exit limits.

The credibility of your close determines how the other negotiator reacts to it, as they will not know how close you are to your limit.

By closing, you are letting the other party know that you do not intend to improve on your current offer and it is in their best interest to reach an agreement with you.

However, attempting to close too early can be dangerous. Once you have presented your 'final offer', and it has been rejected, you could find yourself trading further expensive concessions later on, plus having to do so in circumstances where your attempt to close too early has damaged your credibility.

Have you achieved what you wanted? It is best to end the negotiation when you feel that you have achieved what you wanted. Hanging on for more risks something emerging that causes a collapse of the deal.

Don't agree too hastily: Being too eager to agree because the other party has inadvertently offered, or appears to have offered, to meet all your wildest expectations is not necessarily a sensible course of action either. Your reaction may draw their attention to the fact that they have been over-generous, or may lead them to believe that what they are getting is not worth as much as they thought it was. Then, they may look for some way to undo the deal, or if they have already committed to it, they might still create difficulties during its implementation.

Selecting A Method For Closing

There are several methods of closing, although two—the final concession close and the summary close—tend to predominate.

Final concession close

Terminate the bargaining phase by proposing a conditional

traded concession to clinch the deal. You must carefully judge the standard of concession offered: too big, and they may believe you can be pressurised to concede even more; too small, and it may be too insignificant to bring about acceptance.

Summary close: Remind the other negotiator of the concessions you have both made and highlight the benefits to them of acquiescing to the proposed agreement. Then summarise what has been agreed and how far you have moved. Then call for an agreement on the terms you have offered.

Make them realise the extent of the effort you have both put into the negotiation and emphasise the opportunity to reach a mutually acceptable agreement. This method is particularly useful where progress has been difficult.

Adjournment close: Summarise and suggest an adjournment for each negotiator to consider the merits of agreement on the current terms. Specify the duration of the adjournment (hours, days or weeks).

Adjournment will allow the other negotiator time to reach a considered judgement of the implications of accepting/ rejecting the agreement proposed.

Or/Else close: Summarise as above and call for a decision by a specific date with an explicit statement of the consequences (for both parties) of non-agreement.

This is, of course, an ultimatum: 'Accept the offer or else…!' It is likely to provoke hostility in the other party.

Either/Or close: This is a good approach if you are at your budget limits. You present the other negotiator with alternative agreements and they are free to make a decision from among them.

Agreement Can Be Dangerous

Agreement to what is on offer is the last step in the negotiating process. It is the outcome towards which all negotiators work. Once it is within your reach, you feel relief from the tension of the negotiating process and often experience a sense of euphoria. This is a dangerous time. People often believe something was 'agreed' when in fact it was not. Be on your guard. Pay attention to the details of what you agree to.

Agree what you have agreed upon

It is absolutely essential that both parties agree with each other before they leave the table and that the agreement is recorded in an acceptable manner. This is the way to pre-empt subsequent confusion, disagreement and hostility.

Each issue which has been subject to negotiation should be summarised and the summary agreed between the parties. Any terms that could be subject to differences in interpretation should be defined (e.g. generalised terms, such as reasonable, adequate, sufficient, etc.).

For less formal negotiations, a letter documenting the settlement reached should be sent by you to the other party as soon as possible after the close of negotiations.

Disagreement Over Interpretation

The consequences of not confirming what you have agreed, even with people you know and trust, can be horrendous. Any form of dispute which arises later on, perhaps during the implementation of the negotiated agreement, could imply malpractice on your part, even if you are genuinely innocent. The other negotiator will naturally dispute an interpretation of the alleged agreement that they have retrospectively discovered to be to their detriment. Whether openly stated or not, questions as to each party's good faith and real intentions will be raised. Convincing somebody that they really did agree to what has turned out to be a disadvantageous clause in a contract, even if brilliantly presented, may leave them feeling resentful. It may also leave you with the suspicion that they have been trying to take advantage of you and neither outcome is good for your relationship.

Agreements should be completely clarified at the negotiation stage

To avoid the possibility of discord later, confirm in detail what you have agreed to and clarify any potentially contentious points before you leave the negotiating table.

Negotiate what you agreed

If the summary of what you believe has been agreed to causes conflict, then it is necessary to reopen negotiations until you can reach an agreement. A failure to reach full agreement before you implement a deal is as disastrous as trying to implement a deal which has not been agreed to at all.

CHECKLIST FOR CLOSING AND AGREEING

- Decide where and when you intend to stop trading. 'Is it credible? Is it too soon?'

- Have they identified or signalled that an improved offer on your part on some item will trigger agreement to the package? (If not, you must get all of their objections out before trading any more offers.) If yes, consider the final concession close.

- Lead with the summary close and then try the final concession close or vice versa.

- If you are going for a 'final offer', are you serious or is it a bluff? Remember, a final offer increases in credibility the more formal it is, the more senior the person delivering it, the more public the audience, the more specific it is and the more specific the time for acceptance. Bluffing in the 'final offer' can destroy credibility in the current negotiations and in subsequent ones. Do not try to force a 'final offer' under emotional pressure.

- Remember: 'Adjournment' and 'Or/Else' closes have a greater risk in them than 'Final concession' and 'Summary closes' (and 'Either/Or' closes).

- If the close has succeeded: what has been agreed?

- Detail the agreement.

- List all points of explanation, clarification, interpretation and understanding.

- Try to prevent them from leaving until an agreed summary has been recorded.

- If there is disagreement on an alleged agreement, recommence the negotiation until agreement is reached again.

- If the agreement is oral, send a written note to your opponent of what you believe was agreed immediately after the meeting.

Common Mistakes:

- Inability to terminate bargaining
- Giving away concessions in the euphoria of the closing moments
- Misjudging 'final' offers
- Bluffing with a 'final' offer
- Unconditional closing concessions
- Making large closing concessions
- Not summarising what has been agreed
- Making inappropriate threats using the 'Or/Else' close or the 'Either/Or' close
- Not recording what has been 'agreed' in an acceptable form
- Trying to 'cheat' when recording the alleged agreement

3

Styles Of Negotiation

We do not negotiate in a vacuum. Just because we happen to be deciding something, neither of us need attempt to bargain.

Neither of us need hold any belief in 'fairness'. You might attempt to exploit me by smart sales techniques, by playing on my ignorance, or by threatening me with awful consequences if I resist you.

Where does this leave the negotiator, the person who wants to trade to arrive at a solution when up against somebody else who does not?

THE STYLE DIMENSION: THE RED STYLISTS AND THE BLUE STYLISTS

Negotiators are divided between those who want to take something for nothing (the Red stylists) and those who prefer to trade something for something (the Blue stylists).

The style dimension is a continuum, with aggressive Red stylists at one end and assertive Blue stylists at the other. In between the extremes, there are varying shades of red, purple and blue.

Red stylists believe that negotiations work best for them by:

- seeing all negotiations as 'one-off' activities.
- winning through domination.
- believing that more for them means less for you.
- using bluffs, ploys, 'dirty tricks' and coercion to get their own way.
- taking something for nothing.

Blue stylists believe that negotiations work best for both parties by:

- seeing all negotiations in their long-term contexts.
- succeeding through cooperation.
- believing that more for you means more for them.
- avoiding manipulative techniques.
- addressing each party's interests.
- trading something for something.

In practice, the clash between Red and Blue stylists leads to varying outcomes.

Varying Outcomes

A negotiator can be intimidated into submission by an overtly aggressive Red stylist.

The submissive negotiator in practice gives something for nothing—they give up what the other negotiator wants to take and get nothing in return for it. They are so determined to reach an agreement that they sacrifice their own wants to secure it. They fear failure more than they fear exploitation.

A negotiator can sometimes achieve something for nothing by stealth and by hiding their Red intentions.

These people are covert Red stylists. They exploit either by design or by accident—they cannot resist the opportunity to get something for nothing.

The assertive Blue negotiator, however, always aims to secure an agreement by trading something for something.

In different contexts, you might display behaviour of a particular style. For example:

- Whenever you make an unconditional offer, you are being submissive.

- Whenever you make a unilateral demand, with no offer of anything in return, you are being aggressive.

- When you exploit somebody because you cannot resist the temptation, you are being covert.

- When you use conditional proposals only ('If you... then I...'), you are being assertive.

Thus you require a method of dealing with all of these versions of Red and Blue styles. But you must recognise that while some people are predominantly of one distinct style or the other (it is not difficult to spot an aggressive negotiator!), the majority of people with whom you will negotiate may not be so obvious in their style preferences and might switch between them depending on how they read the situations.

Sometimes you are bound to feel that almost all other negotiators are being difficult to some degree—they do not agree with your solution and stubbornly persist in presenting their own. Most of the time, we manage to rise above our impatience.

But we do have to deal with people who choose to behave in an extremely difficult fashion beyond the temporary irritation of our discovering that they are not overly enthusiastic about our solutions. These people are usually aggressive, bad-mannered and threatening.

The problem is that you want to negotiate and they do not. Their solution requires you to give in by giving them what they want (all of it) and forgoing anything in return.

Break The Connection Between Winning And Intimidation

Not all negotiators behave aggressively because they know that the submissive submit to aggression.

Many of them behave aggressively because they confuse aggression with toughness. They adopt aggressive behaviour because they know of no other method that would get them what they want. And because they find that other people submit to their aggressiveness, they conclude that the aggressive win and therefore they become aggressive whenever they want something.

You have to break the connection between winning and

intimidation. If you do not do this, your submission reinforces the high success rate for those who win through intimidation.

You must find some way to grab their attention and assert two things.

- You will not submit to their intimidation, bullying or threats.
- The only two ways in which they are going to get anything from you are based on either the merits of their case or trading something that you want from them.

If their case has merits (you are wrong on something), it is pointless trying to defend the indefensible—it only fuels their aggression. How you put it right depends on the context, but certainly an indicated willingness to put it right is a step towards doing so.

For example, an irate customer can at least be calmed down by asserting:

- that you are sorry for the stress you have caused them.
- that you will listen to what they have to say.
- that you intend to put the matter right.

In the absence of any merits in their case (which, of course, requires that you listen to what they have to say), or a willingness on their part to consider a trade, you will steadfastly refuse to be bullied.

When confronted by a difficult negotiator, you can style match, but it is risky. In matching, you respond in a similar vein to the aggressive negotiator's behaviour.

The danger is that the aggressive negotiator, interprets your counter-stance merely as you being aggressive too (he misses the message about merits or trading as your preferred solutions) and concludes that it needs an 'extra push' from him to force you into submission. He escalates the pressure and you escalate your response.

This risks a dispute about 'who started it', which blocks progress in the negotiations (even precludes negotiations) because the answer is lost in the confusing layers of mutual insults, threats and counters. The outcome depends on what happens after your bout of style matching.

You style match to avoid submitting to aggressive pressure, but while doing so you must leave wide open the alternative route to a settlement through negotiation. 'It does not have to be this way' is a useful common refrain.

Style contrasting is also risky because a contrasting response to aggression could be perceived by the difficult negotiator as evidence of your submission and a justification for their aggression.

Instead of responding in kind to their ill-mannered and abusive behaviour, you should:
- speak more quietly than they do.
- speak more slowly than they do.
- give way to their interruptions—but pause for a few seconds each time they finish.
- not join in bouts of swearing.
- not get dragged into attack against ascribed motives.
- avoid defending yourself against ascribed motives.
- ignore all threats.

Of course, contrasting responses like these run the risk of being misinterpreted. You could be thought of as submissive. But the contrary impression depends on what else you do in your contrasting style.

You should repeat the statement—having gained their attention, which will probably mean that you have to repeat it more than once—that you will not submit to pressure but only to the merits of their case or to the exchange principle.

For a contrasting style to have an impact, it is absolutely essential that you respond instantly, positively and specifically, and without rancour for past insults, etc., to any and all of the trading moves that they make. This is critical. Delaying your response, being mealy-mouthed endangers the impact of your message. This is particularly true when they make a small signal of a change in tack in the midst of their aggressive mode.

As for their Red moves, you have nothing to gain from responding to them other than to say 'No'. You must affirm whenever appropriate the two principles on which you will agree to a solution (merits of the case and trading).

Your assertive Blue message will eventually prevail (it is the only way they can do business with you).

To help you to hold the line in a difficult and trying situation, remember that toughness is not a synonym for shouting abuse, threatening and intimidation. Toughness is based on an absolute and patient firmness of purpose.

The main problem is that most covert Red stylists do not start off with the intention of cheating you (some do, of course). The majority of occasions when you are exposed to a covert Red, who cheats you, are when otherwise normally honest people find it impossible to resist the temptation to do so. The opportunity to cheat appears without warning and, faced with a safe 'steal', they submit to the temptation.

Opportunity To Cheat

The covert Red and the assertive Blue are easily confused. The fact is that you do not know for certain whether a negotiator will exploit you. They are unaware themselves of how they will act if they are given an opportunity to exploit you.

This puts you at a disadvantage, but this is one disadvantage which is an integral aspect of the business of negotiation. If it is any comfort, it also puts everybody else at a disadvantage—they do not know whether you will be tempted to cheat them. Nobody knows for sure how they will react if an opportunity arises with some person they are dealing with—we all have the potential to be tempted into being covert Red in certain circumstances and we all, almost certainly, have succumbed to that temptation some time or the other.

Hence, you could be dealing with an apparent assertive Blue negotiator behaving just like you.

This person may intend from the start to exploit you or may be unable to resist the temptation. If they intend to exploit you, there are precious few clues, if any, in their behaviour because their intentions are deliberately hidden (that is why they are covert). In the latter case, they cannot help it when the opportunity arises, perhaps on this single occasion. Their behaviour up to that moment is absolutely honest and above-board but they switch to the covert Red behaviour without revealing what they are doing.

Causes Of The Covert Red Problem

The problem can only arise if you have an assertive Blue style and forget to apply the exchange principle based on conditionality.

If you believe that you are dealing with another assertive Blue, you might demonstrate a cooperative tendency in your style and inadvertently expose yourself to exploitation.

If you reveal your expectations—even your interests—believing that it is safe to do so with this person (who is clearly not an aggressive Red stylist), you might create the irresistible temptation for them to take advantage.

If you carelessly offer movement on the implicit understanding that they will reciprocate, that could be an invitation for them to strike. For example:

- You reveal that you desperately require their services—to exploit you, they can increase their entry price.

- You let them know that your budget is in surplus with no provisions—they can take advantage of your predicament by quoting a premium price despite your early payment.

- You confess that your cash flow situation is desperate—they strike swiftly by insisting (with regrets) on advance payment.

Most covert Red responses are accepted by their victims because it is easier to become a submissive Blue, particularly as covert Reds usually dress up their response in such a way as to convince you that they are genuine.

How To Test For Covert Red With Signals

Never become deluded that it is safe to reveal your vulnerabilities and never drop an assertive Blue stance that everything but everything is traded and nothing but nothing is conceded.

Among the assertive skills that you must practise is the use of signals to test for covert Red intentions in people who might be tempted to cheat.

Signals are Blue moves. A major strategic question of all negotiators: How can we indicate a willingness to move without it being interpreted as our giving in? Signals indicate a willingness to consider some form of movement only if that movement is not interpreted as you giving in. For example:

- From demanding full compensation, you signal that you require some compensation.

- From rejecting a demand as impossible, you signal that it would be contrary to normal policy.

- From rejecting a general principle, you signal a willingness to discuss specific instances where it might be applicable.

The key is in how the other negotiator responds to your signal. If they rubbish it, they are revealed to be negotiating as Red stylists. But even if they respond positively to your signal, you still cannot be sure about them. Suppose their clarification questions lead you into further disclosures rather than to a positive response from them.

In short, no matter what they appear to be, you never know if they are genuinely assertive Blue or potentially covert Red.

Responding to your signals might reveal them to be Red stylists (seeking something for nothing) but it will not prove beyond doubt that they are not covert Red stylists who might finesse something for nothing from you if you carelessly give them the chance.

The Exchange Principle

What you do in a negotiation is critical to the outcome. You need not always be a victim of Red stylists. The answer to Red style behaviour lies in your application of the exchange principle.

Every one of us has a Red side because if somebody offers us what we want for nothing, we will surely take it and taking something for nothing is Red-Style behaviour. When we get something for nothing, no exchange takes place.

Now suppose we make a proposal that only consists of stating what we want and offer nothing in return to the other negotiator.

What is the nature of our proposal? Surely an aggressive Red stylist attempts to get something for nothing!

Most of us have a submissive Blue side because there are occasions on which we would certainly offer something and expect nothing in return. Our motivations (love, terror, tiredness and altruism, etc.) are not relevant here.

Now suppose we make a proposal that only consists of an offer (which gives them what they want) and requires nothing at all from the other negotiator.

What is the nature of this proposal? Surely a submissive Blue stylist's way of giving away something for nothing! And when we give something for nothing, no exchange takes place.

Thus, these types of proposals by themselves identify the aggressive Red or the submissive Blue stylist. Separately, they are unhelpful to a negotiator—Red demands provoke resentment if not resistance; Blue offers provoke exploitation.

But the exchange principle combines the Red demand with the Blue offer and together they become the foundation of sound negotiation practice.

Combine condition and offer together into a conditional proposal and the assertive Blue negotiator is totally protected, whatever the style being shown from across the table—overt, covert or submissive.

Analogously, the two elements, sodium and chlorine, are poisonous to humans if ingested separately, but they are also the foundation of life (salt) when ingested together.

The Purple Style

Think of the assertive conditional proposal as a Purple style (a bit of Red and a bit of Blue—the proportions depending on the terms of a proposed deal).

Conditional proposals consisting of your Red conditions and your Blue offers are Purple defences against any Red plays, whether openly aggressive or covertly threatening.

Your imposed conditionality asserts that they cannot get what they want from you without you getting what you want from them.

The exchange principle conditionally:

- blocks aggressive Red stylists from intimidating you into submission for as long as you apply it.

- does not exploit the submissive Blue because being used to giving things away for nothing they get something back through your conditional offer.

- paralyses the covert Red because if they challenge the exchange principle (you must get something back for what you offer them), they would have to reveal their Red 'something for nothing' intentions, which the covert cannot do.

- is acceptable in form at least if not in its content by genuine assertive Blue negotiators because they apply the same Purple exchange principle themselves in their negotiations.

CHECKLIST
FOR NEGOTIATION STYLES

- 'More for me means less for you' is a Red style.
- 'More for me means more for you' is a Blue style.
- Aggressive Red stylists take something for nothing.
- Submissive Blue stylists give something for nothing.
- Covert Red stylists finesse something for nothing.
- Assertive Blue stylists trade something for another.
- Against aggressive Red stylists: assert that you will not submit to intimidation. Agreement is only possible if it is based on either the merits of the case or the exchange principle.
- Apply the Purple exchange principle to all proposals.

Common Mistakes:
- Being inflexible when dealing with styles
- Submitting to aggressive Red behaviour
- Failing to test for covert Red responses to signals
- Forgetting to link your Red conditions with your Blue offers

4

Role Of Ploys

For a lot of people, negotiation is about 'dirty tricks', 'ploys' and 'gambits', which are sometimes confused with tactics. However, much of the advice available on ploys and tricks is unhelpful.

While learning about manipulative approaches to negotiation has something to commend it—because any experience of business negotiation will show numerous ploys being tried upon you—refining your manipulation skills has little to commend it. But because negotiation is an unscripted interaction with no rules, no appeals and no comebacks, it appears on the surface that a manipulative approach is the dominant one and something you must become adept at quickly if you are to do well.

The fact remains that manipulative approaches can be counter-productive, if you confuse identifying 'what some people might try to do to you' in a negotiation with 'what you must learn to do to them.'

Beware:
- You forget the appropriate ploy for the situation
- You apply the wrong ploy for the situation

This could leave you bereft of ideas when trying to develop a negotiation plan or trying to conduct a negotiation.

A ploy identified by you in the course of a negotiating exchange is a ploy neutralised. Moreover, the fact that you realise that they are attempting to manipulate you, should alert you to their Red intentions.

Role Of Manipulative Ploys

All manipulative ploys have a single aim, namely, to influence the perception you have about the other's power relative to your own.

Your perceptions of their power and your expectations of the likely outcome of the negotiation are linked.

- The less power relative to yours that you perceive them to have, the greater your expectation that the outcome will be favourable to you.

- The more power that you perceive them to have relative to yours, the less your expectation that the outcome will be favourable to you.

The manipulative negotiator strives to influence your perceptions of their power relative to yours because by doing so he can directly influence what you expect to result from the negotiation.

If you perceive your power to be:

- non-existent in the situation, you are likely to give in (which happens every time you visit a supermarket to buy some groceries).

- balanced with theirs, you are likely to trade.
- overwhelming, you are likely to impose compliance on them. (Why negotiate if they have no options?)

All manipulative ploys can be assigned predominantly to three main stages or tasks in a negotiation.

- Dominating
- Shaping
- Closing

Negotiations generally follow the above sequence.

Dominance

In the dominance stage, the manipulator works to dominate you and the proceedings. If he manages to take over the negotiations in this way, he can exert great psychological pressure on you. Knowing that this is his purpose, you should arm yourself against being taken for a ride.

Insist on preconditions before negotiating

You must decide whether you are willing to accept the pre-conditions. You can assert that 'nothing is ruled in and nothing is ruled out', and that you would find it difficult to make progress with 'one arm tied behind your back', or that you have a counter-set of preconditions which are chosen to circumscribe his room for manoeuvre.

Declare some issues non-negotiable

Issues that are claimed to be non-negotiable can be divided

into two: those that are genuinely non-negotiable and those that are motivated by an attempt to weaken your stance.

Where there is some pressing emotional reason for making some issues non-negotiable, you can assert your belief that the issues should be a part of the eventual deal, but to assist the exploration of what both of you want, you are willing to have these issues aside for the moment. Depending on the progress on the other issues, you can raise the non-negotiable issues at a later time on the grounds that they are the only remaining obstacles to an overall agreement.

Attempt unilaterally to determine the agenda, its order and timing

Seizing control of the agenda (the issues that can be discussed and the order in which issues are to be discussed) is a common manipulative device, and not just in negotiations. The difference between negotiations and routine meetings ensures at least a base for resisting this type of manipulation.

Nothing can really be negotiated without the consent of both parties. Agreeing what to negotiate and in what order is a necessary part of a negotiation taking place. Where the manipulator scores with this ploy, it is usually by default.

Behave in an aggressive 'Red' style

The aggressive Red style can be tackled using the methods against the use of threats of sanctions. There is little point in responding to threats, especially counter-threats, as this feeds the emotional commitment of the aggressive person. One of the most successful techniques for dealing with threats is to ignore them and with deadlines is to not acknowledge them.

Disdainfully dismiss you, your products, business and views

The dismissal of you, your products, business and beliefs, etc., is an attempt to provoke you into anger or to belittle you and whatever power you feel you have. Again, by remembering that the purpose of the manipulator's behaviour is to affect your perceptions of the power balance, you can disarm the manipulative ploy by not letting it get through to you.

Intimidation with props

They may try to intimidate you with props, such as plush offices, evidence of power, humiliating circumstances for the meeting, keeping you waiting, etc.

As for intimidation through props, you can cope with them by remembering that 'all that glitters is not gold'. It is when you take on board the subliminal message—this negotiator is too rich and powerful for me to expect too much—that you are making your most serious concession, especially if you start to negotiate with yourself and lower your sights.

Shaping

In the second stage of negotiation, the manipulator works to shape the deal in his favour. Most deals can be cut numerous ways and by shaping each aspect of the deal, the manipulator is picking up benefits—often without giving anything in return—that could more appropriately be held on to or traded for something else.

Tough guy/soft guy

It does not require two people to play this ploy. It can be as easily (and less obviously) played by one person. He is on your side, he says, but he has people to report to, who do not see you in the same light. However, if you give him something here and something there, he will have a better chance of getting the deal past them.

If you believe him, you cut here and there and over there. The deal shapes up into a one-way street—for his benefit, not yours.

You can counter with your own 'tough-nice guy' routine—you too have difficult people to please, hence you need something back for any moves that you make.

You can also reveal your knowledge of the ploy, perhaps humorously and refuse any movement without a trade.

Salami syndrome

Shape by cutting thin slices at a time. Unable to get you to move the whole hog in one go, they get you to agree a little here and there. Once that is agreed, they expand on the movement they have gained.

You can simply salami back—this little movement costs them this little amount, that extended (bigger) movement costs them this bigger amount.

When a deal is being implemented, salami can take on a vicious form, sometimes called the 'nibble'. Here the other negotiator tries to bend the deal by nibbling away at the conditions they did not like at the time.

For example, you thought they had agreed to thirty days payment but they keep taking forty days to pay. Over time, the nibbles get out of control and establish legitimacy because what started off as a tiny nibble can become a permanent and expensive shift in the terms of the deal and very difficult to reverse.

The best thing to do with nibbles is to stamp on them immediately, when they appear, no matter how small the initial transgression. If they agree to pay in thirty days, require a condition that failure to do so would incur a penalty. If they have no intention of nibbling, they will not demur at a penalty—if they do, you have been warned.

Add-on

The possibility of an add-on ploy is always present. You thought the price was inclusive, but once you agree to the price, add-ons spring up like weeds. It's extra for this and extra for that. The true cost mounts, which is particularly disconcerting when the add-ons are revealed afterwards when you need some service that you thought was included in the deal.

The add-on is the special favourite of the covert Red negotiator. It can turn a moderately lucrative deal into a virtual licence to collect money. Be wary is the best advice. Always ask for a clear statement of what exactly is included in the proposed deal and what is excluded.

They love you and your product but cannot reach the price and there is no way round their budget constraint. The cupboard is bare, etc. When done convincingly, you reshape your exit terms to secure the deal. They get what they want.

You get less than you expected.

Counters are difficult—you can test the constraints, but it is probably better to decide early on that. If you can make a deal with this negotiator, fine, but if you can't you are perfectly relaxed about not doing any deal. It is always bad business to cross a bottom line in hot pursuit.

Closing

In the final closing stage, the manipulator works to close the deal on his terms. He uses time pressure frequently, playing on some notional deadline common to you both or credible to you.

There is also the problem that because one of the important costs of negotiations is the time they take, which prevents you from doing other things, the plausibility of getting the deal settled quickly is persuasive.

Rushed ideas are bad deals. If somebody is hustling you to close, it might be because the deal suits them as it stands more than it suits you.

Demand that you split the difference

This gets you halfway across the gap between you both and has a pressing, though spurious, logic about it. If you both move halfway, then what could be a fairer compromise? That depends, on the nature of the gap between you. Has the manipulator arrived at the gap by falsely padding his entry position, while you were less devious and are closer to your exit?

If the pressure to secure the deal accompanies the 'split the difference' ploy, it can prove irresistible. To avoid the ploy, try to work in gaps of those which are not easily split. A gap of ten is easily conceived of five each; a gap of 11.3 is not so obviously divided.

Claim it: 'Now or never'

'There is a tide in the affairs of men...' Whether it really is the last chance to secure a deal is a question worth asking. The context might suggest otherwise. You can only judge the circumstances as you see them. One question to ask is: Why? The answer might give you a clue to the credibility of the claim.

Threaten with the 'or/else' close

If credible, you must make a choice. Perhaps, you should be generating options during a negotiation that give you negotiating room. The more options you have, the stronger your position.

By identifying the likely ploys (and there are many more than the selection quoted above), you can win the battle to influence your perceptions.

If you know what he is about, it makes it easier either to:

- counter (every ploy has a counter), or
- ignore (any ploy is weakened by being ignored).

If your perceptions are uninfluenced by the manipulator, you can concentrate on negotiating the issues.

CHECKLIST FOR MANIPULATIVE PLOYS

- All ploys have counters.
- A ploy recognised is a ploy disarmed.
- Ploys are to be avoided in the interests of longer-term relationships.
- Ploys aim to influence your perceptions.
- Your expectations of the outcome are influenced by your perceptions of their powers.
- Check out changes in your perceptions.
- Which of the three stages are you in: dominating, shaping, closing?

Common Mistakes:

- Ploys
- Gambits
- Dirty tricks
- Dishonesty

Negotiating
Disputes

'The best way to lose a friend is by bargaining with him.'
—Russian proverb

Intractable disputes are unlikely to be solved by negotiation
—which is why they are intractable. But not all disputes—
even some bitter ones—need become intractable. It depends
on what the parties do once the dispute is recognised.

There is a continuum from giving in when faced with
a dispute to using violence to force them to give in. In
between there are many alternatives to violence. The parties
themselves can attempt to resolve the dispute by private
discussion, negotiation, mediation or problem solving.
They can appeal to private third parties for arbitration or
for a command decision.

When many of us think of negotiating in a difficult situation,
we think of sitting across the table from a cold, calculating,
crafty adversary bent on maximising personal benefit.

While such a situation can indeed be challenging, skilled
negotiators often report that they are the most unsettled

when they encounter a colleague, friend or family member across the proverbial bargaining table.

So, why is this? And, more importantly, how do we effectively and respectfully negotiate with individuals close to us? In order to get an answer, we must first reflect upon the angst often associated with such negotiations.

INABILITY TO ADDRESS A DISPUTE AS AN ISOLATED MATTER

Negotiating with those close to us is further complicated by the fact that a dispute between connected parties is often understood in the context of previous dealings and as a harbinger of future interactions. As a result, relatively 'minor' matters may be surprisingly significant to one or more parties. Also, what might appear to a disinterested party to be a simple resolution may be wholly unsatisfactory to a connected party. To further complicate matters, closely connected parties often use one disagreement as a surrogate for another dispute that may be too uncomfortable to address.

Another significant challenge in negotiations between connected parties is the readiness of one or more parties to quickly cede his or her interests so as to please or benefit the other party, or to be perceived as generous, kind, etc. We have all heard the refrain, 'I'm fine with whatever you want...'

While capitulation does indeed smoothen the immediate dispute, there may be unintended consequences. Failing to work through disputes in business and family relationships often compromises our ability to reach mutually satisfactory and durable resolutions.

The starting point for the engagement is to acknowledge the situation. A potential opening might sound like this: I value our relationship and respect that you have a different perspective. I do not want our dispute to get any worse or for it to remain unresolved.

Focus On Interests, Not Positions

Skilled negotiators seek to identify 'interests' in order to resolve disputes in a way that meets both parties' needs. By contrast, ineffective negotiators tend to argue their case and speak in terms of 'positions' that tend to be all-or-nothing propositions. This 'winner-take-all' approach is particularly damaging in close relationships.

We negotiate best if we seek a third option that meets all the parties' interests, rather than by resolutely maintaining our position or simply capitulating.

The three components of dispute resolution are power, rights and interests. Power in this context is coercion. Rights are independent standards of fairness supported by law or social conventions. Interests are perceived needs, concerns and fears. These components are all-pervasive; they are present in all disputes.

Most disputes are settled amicably between private parties without resorting to litigation or violence. A major cost of negotiations is the time they take. Therefore, they are mostly less costly than litigation or violence.

Some business sectors have endemic dispute relationships. In construction, for example, main contractors drive down prices for work from subcontractors (often using aggressive Red ploys); the subcontractors, to make a profit, often skimp on performance (using covert Red ploys); the main contractors, to avoid fraud, delay payments to subcontractors until they have checked everything; to survive, the subcontracts skimp on their work. The result is an industry riddled with contentious claims for extra work done (and contentious people pursuing them) and counter-claims for non-performance, both of which wind their way slowly into arbitration and legal procedures.

ESCALATION OF CONFLICT

Disputes can escalate from a difference of opinion over some problem into a major crisis. What begins with some low-scale anxiety ends with bitter feelings of revenge.

The deadening spiral of conflict escalation is at the root of most intractable disputes. Once the problem emerges (perhaps as seen by an affected party), it can pass into a partisans assertion of one group's right over another's. Sides are taken; and those who feel stronger, whip up the fears and anxieties of those likely to be influenced.

Polarisation leads to militant hostility towards people holding a different view, including people from within the affected group who are cast as 'traitors', 'spies' or 'enemies'. Soon, all restraint is lost. Moderate appeals and people are pushed aside as being 'soft' on the issues.

Threats escalate as perceptions of what is realistically possible becomes unrecognisably distorted. The original issue is now shrouded in the history of the relationship of the disputing parties. Whatever one did or did not do, it is impossible to separate the issue from the behaviour of the parties. Intractability reigns, perhaps to the mutual destruction of both parties.

Interests

Interests are fundamental to the negotiator's quest to resolve a difficult dispute. Interests express the needs, concerns and fears of the parties. They are what motivate you to want something. Behind all of your wants in a negotiation stand your interests.

In a majority of negotiations, consideration of what people want is sufficient to result in an agreement. Negotiators are able to resolve their disputes (who gets how much of what, where and when) without recourse to uncovering their interests or those of the people with whom they negotiate.

Complex disputes cannot be settled solely by addressing the expressed wants of the parties (and it can take some effort even to uncover other people's wants. This is especially true when they have many wants because this reflects the fact that they may have competing interests. Leaving the forbidden or disregarded, removes the chance of using revealed interests to promote a settlement.

The Negotiator-As-Mediator

Mediation usually involves some form of impartial intervention by a neutral third party, who cannot impose a settlement but can assist the parties to secure one.

Mediators are often used when negotiations cannot close the gap between the negotiators' own efforts. Basically, the mediator goes behind the public stances of the negotiators, confidentially assesses their interests and finds out their exit positions on the issues. When there are sufficient overlaps or closeness of issues, a mutually acceptable settlement is possible; the mediator recommends that they try again.

Negotiators find it difficult to rise above the fray when head-to-head in a dispute and for practical reasons there are just not enough mediators to go round, even assuming both parties would consider using a mediator's services or could afford to do so.

The negotiator who understands the process of negotiation and the appropriate approach to take with difficult negotiators can engage in the unusual role of the negotiator-as-mediator. The negotiator-as-mediator differs from the normal mediator. For a start, negotiators are hardly impartial and neutral. They are partisans to their own wants and interests. They cannot expect to get behind the public stances of the other negotiator, nor will they be able to receive confidential briefings on the other negotiator's exit positions.

But faced with a dispute that is heading towards deadlock, if not quite intractability, the negotiator can adapt some techniques of the mediator and apply them to search for a way towards a settlement with or without the other negotiator's knowledge.

To undertake this task, however, the negotiator has to adopt certain attitudes to the role of the negotiator-as-mediator.

In particular, the negotiator-as-mediator must accept that:

- both parties have interests that are important for them.
- a solution meets as many of the interests of each side as is practicable.
- interests like wants may be traded.
- there is likely to be more than one solution.
- some interests will be competing and others will be compatible.

This approach helps the negotiator-as-mediator to rise above the fray without compromising his role as a negotiator.

Hidden Interests

Getting negotiators to reveal their wants can be difficult. Getting them to reveal their interests is no less easy. This is not necessarily a case of the negotiator being difficult.

They may not know what their interests are. They may not be used to expressing their interests or formulating them in any conscious sense. Why should they? Our wants express what we want, our interests why we want it. And most of us do not examine our motives for what we want.

Others may deliberately hide their interests either because they are ashamed of them or because they hope to gain advantage by not revealing them.

Teachers claiming wage increases seldom do so on the basis that they want the higher living standards enjoyed by others. They usually present wage claims as an investment in the future of our children. Others might manoeuvre against a position on some excuse, when they are really against it, because it will disadvantage them in some way. For example, a resident might lead a campaign against something ostensibly on its merits when in fact they are jealous of the person initiating the project and the promotion they might gain from it being successful.

The negotiator-as-mediator can initiate exploration of each party's interests by basic communication.

- Actively listen to the other negotiator and look for expression of interests (concerns, needs, fear and motives).

- Question to highlight interests.

- Summarise to clarify what lies behind specific wants.

- Reframe the issues to reveal alternative solutions to interests.

Interests And Options

The negotiator-as-mediator does not focus on the declared positions of the other negotiator. This is a cause of deadlock. Simply denying people what they want is a negative approach and it can be perceived as being threatening.

By shifting the emphasis on to why they want something (their interests), it might be possible to sidestep round the inflexible position and consider other options.

Generating new options is a useful way to break through the deadlock. If linked to perceptive assessments of their interests, progress can be made in finding a solution. Having identified an interest, the next important step is to engage with them in searching for other solutions.

To assist this process, the negotiator-as-mediator tries to set standards by which options will be discussed (better by example than initially by precept because the negotiator's motives may be challenged).

A common cause of failure in searching for new options is that of the negotiators making premature judgements about what is proposed or tentatively suggested. Brainstorming techniques are useful here. Separating the process of inventing new options from judging them, helps otherwise fragile new ideas survive long enough to be seriously considered, which could mean that they themselves lead to other options which are more credible.

The negotiator strives constantly to challenge the view that the only solution possible is the impossible one that is driving the negotiators into a deadlock. Retreating into defences based on denying that there is a problem with the single option on the table, or asserting that if there is a problem it is not one shared by you, is utterly counter-productive. If deadlock is a problem, then the solution that is creating that deadlock is a problem, too. A cooperative effort to create some new options is worthwhile for both negotiators.

Values

By putting yourself in their position, if only as a mind game—without adopting their positions, but trying to see why they have adopted them—can reveal underlying value differences. Behind interests stand a person's values.

Values are the belief systems that give people their views of the world, how it works and their place in it. They take a long time to emerge and are usually very difficult to shift once they are entrenched.

In a clash of values, the negotiator faces the most difficult of all deadlocks. Any attempts that are perceived to change somebody's values are bitterly resisted. If a dispute can be escalated into a struggle of values, the spiral of conflict can be spun rapidly into total opposition. This leads to clear advice: understand a negotiator's values, even study them, but make no moves to challenge them in any way.

This creates problems when we are not sure of the other negotiator's values. This is yet another reason for listening to what the other negotiators say, how they say it, the specific words used, the phrases and clichés scattered in their sentences and any stereotypes they let slip. These will reflect their values.

Be wary of springing to the defence of your own values. It is better to acknowledge the clear differences in values in a non-threatening and non-condemnatory way. This is especially true when dealing across cultures, in countries other than the one with which you are familiar. The more you know about the other negotiator's values in a deadlock situation, the more likely you are to avoid the sort of misunderstandings that lead to avoidable disputes.

If you want to do business with a country where you are a foreigner, it is best that you remember that your political views are only relevant where you vote, that your religion is between you and your maker, that your moral code is between you and your life partner, that your ethics are between you and your legal system, and that what else goes on in that country is none of your business—if you want to do business there.

Emotions

Of course, emotional considerations are not avoidable. In disputes, they arise inevitably from the commitment each negotiator has to their preferred solution. The question centres on how they should be handled.

Recognising somebody's emotions is an obvious first step to recognise that they have the right to feel emotional about something as you do. Telling somebody that you feel something about an event (for instance, an apparent slur) might be enough to prevent its reoccurrence. True, they might take advantage of your revelation and mock you. This at least tells you what you are dealing with. But asserting their legitimacy to express emotions in the negotiations might help build a bridge between you.

Negotiators sometimes express themselves abrasively because they feel intensely about something. They might also do this as part of their efforts to dominate you. Because you are not going to be fazed in the slightest by dominating behaviour, you are not going to react emotionally to their emotional outbursts. You need not retaliate with an emotional display of your own. You understand that they have the right to be emotional without you having to agree that they are right to insist on their solution.

It always comes down to what you do next. If you are the cause of their emotional outburst, apologise for the unintended action (remember the merits of their case) and graciously accept their apologies if the situation is reversed.

CHECKLIST FOR
DIFFICULT DISPUTES

- Adopt the 'negotiator-as-mediator' role.
- Search for their interests as the motivators of their wants.
- Use debate techniques to uncover hidden interests.
- Search for their values.
- Do not challenge, criticise or threaten the other negotiator's values.
- Understand their values as the cause of their motivations (interests).
- Generate new options by refraining from premature judgement of proposed solutions.
- Seek agreement on the substantive issues using new options to meet each party's interests.

Common Mistakes:

- Ignoring the role of interests in generating wants
- Preferring the satisfaction of mutual failure to the successful conclusion of a dispute
- Attacking the other negotiator's values
- Instantly rejecting attempts to discover new options

PERFECT APPRAISAL

Performance appraisal is the process of evaluating and documenting one's performance on the job. It is part of career development. This book deals with the appraisal process, training for appraisal, pitfalls in appraisal and the dos and don'ts of appraisal.

Perfect Appraisal provides simple techniques to a perfect appraisal with a holistic approach.

PERFECT ASSERTIVENESS

Assertiveness is important in all forms of communication. It is a way of relating to others that respects both your own and other people's needs, wants and rights. Aggressiveness provokes counter-aggression, assertiveness doesn't. This book spells out assertiveness training, responses—passive, aggressive and assertive, effective communication, assertiveness skills and the benefits of being assertive.

Perfect Assertiveness helps you understand assertiveness as a life skill.

PERFECT COMMUNICATION

Communication is the process of sharing information, knowledge or meaning. What matters most is the 'response-ability'; response is more important than the message. Listeners must not just hear; they must listen. This book deals with speaking skills, writing skills and listening skills.

Perfect Communication is much more than just this.

PERFECT CV

A curriculum vitae (CV) or résumé presents a record of your qualities, skills and experience to an employer, so that your suitability for a particular job can be assessed. In Latin, 'curriculum vitae' means 'the way your life has run' and 'résumé' is the French word for 'summary'. This book deals with making a CV special, writing a CV with lack of experience, tailoring a CV and digital and online CVs.

Perfect CV helps you to compile your CV and suggests ways to improve it.

PERFECT LEADER

If you want to inspire, motivate and engage, and move people into action, leadership is the ability you require. Leaders set direction and develop the skill to guide people to the right destination. This book spells out leadership styles, initiatives that are needed, proactive tools, the importance of perseverance and methods to step out of the comfort zone.

Perfect Leader helps you to inspire the vision of the future as a leader. It equips you to make strategic decisions, shape conflict and find your competitive edge.

PERFECT MEETING

Meetings help one to build rapport. They are a forum for inter-learning and understanding; a platform to share information. *Perfect Meeting* is about the basic skills of management. This book deals with effective meetings, conference meetings, stand-up meetings, one-on-one meetings and the tasks and skills of the chairperson.

Perfect Meeting helps you generate cooperation and commitment to attain higher levels of performance.

PERFECT PRESENTATION

Presentation skills are critical as they help one to inform, motivate and inspire others. It is a means to get a message across to the listeners, with a persuasive element. This book talks about the canons of persuasive presentations, verbal and non-verbal communication, styles of presentation and the opening and closing of a presentation.

Perfect Presentation helps you master the art of making effective presentations.

www.ingramcontent.com/pod-product-compliance
Lightning Source LLC
Chambersburg PA
CBHW030849090426
42737CB00009B/1160